Unity Village - 07

Judy, I appreciate

just the way you are!

In His service,

Pearl

On Any Given Day . . .
A Butterfly May
Cross Your Path

On Any Given Day . . . A Butterfly May Cross Your Path

Collective Poetry, Prose, and Thoughts

Carolyn Saunders Banks

VANTAGE PRESS
New York

Illustrations by Autumn L. N. Cobeland

Cover design by Susan Thomas

Published by Vantage Press, Inc.
419 Park Ave. South, New York, NY 10016

Manufactured in the United States of America
ISBN: 0-533-14536-8

Library of Congress Catalog Card No.: 2003090616

0 9 8 7 6 5 4 3 2 1

This Labor of Love is dedicated to:

My Son,
Martin Lawrence Banks, III,
Who read everything I wrote
and provided comments

My Friend,
Lawrence Delano Wilson,
Whose sincere appreciation
and constant encouragement
spurred me to action
January 1, 2000

To The Readers:

On any Given Day . . .
   A Butterfly May Cross Your Path So

May The Wind
of the Spirit

Blow God's Presence
Into Your Life . . .

Whisper God's Love
Into Your Heart . . .

Breathe God's Promise
Into Your Being . . .

As You Await
Your Miracle.

The Author—A Self Portrait, Third Person

*Caring
  *Believes in prayer
    *Seeks the Lord
      *Willing vessel
        *Committed to the Lord's works
          *Struggles with patience

*Whatever her problems, she will put them aside to help
  *Stubborn
    *Quiet
      *Hard working
        *Dry humor
          *Resolute

*Talent to organize or schedule complex events or tasks
  *Phenomenal memory for numbers
    *Gourmet down-home chef
      *Nickname: Songbird
        *Teaching nature
          *Dynamic, energetic hostess

*She believes that every effort should be made to instill
    quality into genuine relationships with friends.
  *Attempts perfectionism
    *Impressive
      *Consistently reliable
        *Perceptive
          *Charismatic personality

Contents

Part 3: Second Thoughts

Part 4: Gracefully Silver

Part 5: Sensitively Pensive

Understanding Each Section

1. Under His Grace

God is awesome! He has given each of us an abundance of unique talents and abilities to be independent . . . and He loves us anyway.

2. Sharing Friends

Good people are treasures who enrich lives and buoy souls.

The Angel Memorials

He taketh away and creates angels to watch over those left behind. Communication with our angels is accomplished through memories stored in the heart.

3. Second Thoughts

Because of complexity or phenomenal beauty many things in this world demand an additional moment of contemplation.

4. Gracefully Silver

Those who are aged and wintry possess the seeds to plant for spring blossoms to bloom. Thank you.

5. Sensitively Pensive

Delicate reflection can elucidate confusing moments and intensify the desire to hope, to dream and to create.

6. Secret Closet

Communication Central—a place that allows the expression of feelings, supplications and praise to a Mighty God. A place to hear His voice.

Introduction

This book has come together over ten years of actual writing and fifty plus years of highs and lows, joys and disappointments, planned events and unexpected disasters. But through it all, there ran a strand of ethereal support that was sometimes innocuous and at other times boldly apparent.

The world is generally a beautiful place, but it does have a darkened element that must also be acknowledged, however brief. *On Any Given Day . . .* presents many aspects thereof. It was written, gathered, and presented to create a pause from the rat race, or an awareness of a more gentle, thoughtful domain, or a reconnection with a spiritual sense. When most of the inclusions were written, there was no public intent. With the passage of time, limited sharing and gentle nudging, the courage to publish the contents of this book was mustered.

For those who read this book, the hope is that you will enjoy a smile, a peaceful moment, an agreement—possibly even a tear with the discovery of an emphatically honest portrayal of life, from one perspective—mine.

I thank God for my quiet moments with Him. I am also indebted to those family members and true friends who tolerated less than perfect connections during the ambitious undertaking of making everything come together to publish *On Any Given Day . . . A Butterfly May Cross Your Path.*

> As you journey through this life,
> proceeding to secure a miracle,
> take the time to allow
> a butterfly to cross your path.

On Any Given Day . . .
A Butterfly May
Cross Your Path

Part 1

Under His Grace

God is awesome. He has given each of us an abundance of unique talents and abilities to be independent . . . and He loves us anyway.

Praise & Worship—Brief Interrogatives

Praise and worship are important parts of any relationship with God. There are as many different types of acclamation as there are types of people, but there are things that remain constant:

THE WHO?—Preferred Individual—one with a heart, all shape, sizes, colors

THE WHAT?—Resonance—A word, a shout, a prayer, a thought, a chant, a song

THE WHERE?—Any Location—under a roof, under the stars, in broad daylight

THE WHEN?—Daily—morning, noon, night

THE HOW?—With Sincerity—from the heart with animation or placidness

Worship & Praise

Praise Him with your eyes—
  Look on things that are positive,
  good, or have the potential to be.

Praise Him with your smile—
  Let others see the peace, comfort,
  and confidence He has provided.

Praise Him with your hands—
  Work on and for what He has declared.
  Raise not a hand in anger.
  Raise to embrace. Lift to magnify.
  Bring together in appreciation.

Praise Him with your mouth—
  Let His blessings and your thankfulness be
  known in every place.

Praise Him with your feet—
  Dance with sincerity and message.
  Walk in the paths of righteousness.
  Stand by His Word.

Praise Him with all your heart—
  Allow yourself to be an earthen vessel and be
  filled with His goodness.

Praise Him for life, for He gives it every day!

Oh, What a Mighty God!

A Flea—tiny, but totally complete
A Raindrop—powerful when many come together
A Spider—maintains Nature's balance
A Smile—capable of changing a mood
A Breeze—provides unseen relief
A Friend—lends an ear & gives support
A Family—provides sustenance from the very beginning
A Blossom—presents natural beauty
A Star—stirs curiosity & wonder
A Hug—establishes a human connection
A Prayer—communicates with a Mighty God.

We Come

We come as women,
Not yet having met our full potential.
We come seeking . . .
    Your heart, Your mind, Your love, and Your
    blessing.
We come as leaders . . . who follow.
We come as "forced" heads . . . who negotiate.
    As mothers who weep, mates who sustain,
    As singles who search, friends who bolster.
We come lonely, broken, burdened, downtrodden,
    and fatigued . . . continuously juggling our daily
    roles.
We come to be lifted; by prayer, through meditation,
    With togetherness and support for one another,
      While under Your covering . . . We come.

Grant us peace, mercy, strength, patience, awareness,
    and common sense.
We are here to promote sisterhood led by Your teaching.
We claim success in all our endeavors!
We are faithful. We are expectant. We have come.

Praises to God

Praise God with quiet thoughts
Praise God with loud shouts of Hallelujah
Praise God with hands . . .
    raised, clapping, waving.
Praise God with dance and movement
Praise God with soft swaying . . .
    with closed-eyes and meditation.
Praise God by the giving of tithes and offerings.
Praise God by the giving of yourself.
Praise God with song and raised voices.
Praise God by studying, knowing, and following
    the Word.
Praise God by protecting a child and
    respecting a senior.
Praise God in various ways at different times.

    Simply Praise God!

Secure In His Eternal Arms

"Why do they cry?" Sihea asked with concern.
He said that they were human and could not seem to
　　learn
"That you are fine, Sihea, safely tucked here in my
　　arms.
"The life you had has ended and can no longer do you
　　harm.
"I didn't know so many cared; look at all of my friends
　　there.
"I spent so many lonely nights, when none showed love
　　or care."
He said, "I love you, Sihea, dear, you are my special
　　child.
I gave you breath and life down there, now stay with me
　　awhile.
You read my Word, and followed it. You used it as your
　　guide.
You prayed with worship, praise and love, not
　　boastful nor with pride.
You served my church, you fed the poor, you
　　brought souls to be saved.
That's why you're here for just reward, not
　　languishing in a grave.
The Christian road is difficult, not everyone can cope,
You braved the course, relied on faith and never gave
　　up hope.
Rest now, my child, your work is done,
You've done your best, the battle's won.
Welcome, Sihea, to blessings untold
　　prepare to walk my streets of gold."

Woman, on Women

Women! Delight in the Lord for all our special needs.
Women who . . .
>Love the Lord,
>Trust in the Lord,
>Commit to the Lord,
>Pray to the Lord, &
>Hold onto His promises . . .

Are filled with the ability to fulfill the call to be earthly
caregivers to many with . . .
>Patience
>Listening ears
>Smiles
>Joy
>Wisdom
>Hugs
>Suggestions
>Encouragement
>Assistance
>Hope &
>Strength

These things we can offer because the Lord has ordered
our steps. Whether young or old, **He** has given to
us:
Patience
Listening ears
Smiles
Joy
Wisdom
Hugs
Suggestions
Encouragement
Assistance
Hope &
Strength.
The capacity to function beyond fatigue, beyond closed
doors, beyond empty pockets, beyond brick walls,
beyond illness has been bestowed upon us. **He** has
given us the ability to function . . . no matter what!

O God, thank you for making each of us a unique
instrument of caring and intercession. Thank you
for making us Women!

Part 2

Sharing Friends

Section I

Good people are treasures who enrich lives and buoy souls.

Worship Litany—Grateful for a Pastor

Leader: Bless the Lord, O my soul, for a pastor who has brought visions to life and souls into the kingdom.

People: O Lord, we are thankful for Your servant.

Leader: Bless the Lord, O my soul, for years of adversity to grow, and the challenge of laboring in Your fields.

People: O Lord, we are grateful for Your servant.

Leader: We sing praises because the old became new and the edifice expanded.

People: O Lord, we are blessed through Your servant.

Leader: We sing praises, for the flock grew, waned, but grew again for now many know the road to Your kingdom is not through a building.

People: O Lord, we give You adoration for Your servant.

Leader: For ministries that touched prisoners, the homeless, the ailing, and downtrodden, we acknowledge a sense of shepherding and caring.

People: O Lord, we are grateful for Your servant.

Leader: For ministries of enlightenment, conveying to the children the traps of worldly pleasures, providing spirit-directed Bible studies, we respect Your servant's devotion and faithfulness to the Word.

People: O Lord, we magnify Your holy name with Your servant.

Leader: For counseling, prayer and dedication; for speaking in tongues and chanted praise, we recognize a benevolent and compassionate spirit.

People: O Lord, we praise You for Your servant.

Leader: We praise You, our God, for all that has been done for this humanity through your earthen vessel.

People: O Lord, we are grateful for Your servant and pray Your blessings on Him and on Your works done through Him. Amen.

A Christian Family

Caring, loving, supportive, and more,
Christian families are tagged at the door.

Hilarious, lighthearted, whimsical, absurd,
The folks in this grouping acclaim still The Word.

There's a sincerity, a gentleness, a genuine smile,
When greeting each other not seen in a while.

Training the young ones
For the paths they will take,
Respecting the seniors with honor, none fake.

Rejoicing at holidays and traveling to share,
The hope for the future, for the present, to care.

Hardworking and dutiful,
Involved and concerned,
From each other over long years,
Much has been learned.

Marriages last longer, births a shared joy,
Accomplishments applauded—celebrations—oh, boy!

With the feeling of closeness, no hesitation to ask,
When advice is needed to complete a hard task.

Church workers all, in varied duty length,
Remembering always
That the Lord is their strength.

By His stripes, they are consistently healed,
Through prayer for one another,
His plan is revealed.

Thank You, Father, for the Holy Trinity
And for our Christian family
whose affection is free.

Half Notes . . . Quarter Notes . . . My Notes

Who would have thought all those years ago,
that life would have been so sweet?
Who would have thought that all those notes
would hold a sincere sacred beat?
There have been times along the way
when rehearsals and practice were labored.
But because they all sauntered down God's holy path,
taste and tolerance were both sweetly savored.

Being one who loves God, music, people and such,
I suppose there was just one way to go.
To plan choir events every night of the week,
for Music Minister is the title you know.
That means dedication and patience untold.
"Too fast, off beat, what page?"
Comments are heard again and again
from the seniors, men, kids . . . college age.
So why do you do this; oh, man with a job?
Is your forty-hour week not enough?
The answer we get is not what we'd expect,
and may leave us a little rebuffed!

He does what he does because of what's in his heart.
The love of God, music, people, and all.
It takes time and hard work
on the parts of many souls
to help him answer his call.
It descended on him during the sixties revolution,
to give glory, honor, worship and praise;
to our God up above are the voices all gathered
for spirituals, gospel, and hymns to be raised.

It is with heartfelt thanks that we take time to say,
Martin Banks, your labors aren't in vain.
The souls you have saved, or stirred or awakened
for the Kingdom are counted as gain.
Continue, dear friend, husband, lover and mate,
down the road that is so clearly marked.
Though you may not have chosen it,
twenty-nine years ago,
God put His music road map in your heart.

Number One Son

You conquered a mountain, we're humbly quite proud!
You conquered a mountain, we praise God out loud!

It seems so long ago that we left you alone far away.
We took you out to dinner to establish your college stay.
The first words home weren't "Hello, how are you doing?"
Instead it was to let us know that homesickness was
    brewing.
The money was much more than tight. It was simply
    non-existent.
But by the grace of a loving God, bills were paid with
    little resistance.
The teaching staff at our 'Home by the Sea' sent
    challenges that forced your hand.
With determination and fortitude, you made the
    decision to stand.
The mountain grew higher, major courses increased,
The work was unending and the social life ceased.
The darkest moments occurred when choices were made,
For those questionable decisions prolonged time was
    then paid.
You wandered and pondered, motivation you did lack.
Sincere prayers of the saints put you back on the track.
Although one of few males who with the major did stick.
We're proud of that decision and salute your final pick.
You have climbed a rugged mountain and learned much
    along the way,
Your future's filled with positive moments, including
    graduation day.

You conquered a mountain, we're humbly quite proud!
You conquered a mountain, we praise God out loud!

Grandma Memories

Grandma . . . funny hair . . . big smile . . . open arms . . .
Luscious smells drifting from the kitchen.
Keeper of the secret family recipes.
Squeezes that take your breath away.
Special moments saved just for me.

Grandma . . . funny hair . . . big smile . . . open arms . . .
Has all the things Mom doesn't know I need.
Tells me stories from before time was kept.
Tells me again and again how much I've grown.
Has something special for me 'cause she says, "I'm
    special."

Grandma . . . funny hair . . . big smile . . . open arms . . .
Irons clothes on a funny board with legs.
Rocks on the porch while peering at the stars, saying
    nothing.
Makes me not miss cable or video games or WROC.
Commands good behavior from the "grands" without
    even asking.

Grandma . . . funny hair . . . big smile . . . open arms . . .
Timeless, not old . . . energetic, but not speedy . . .
Tasteful, not old fashioned . . . knowledgeable always.
Particular, but not finicky . . . living example and
    role-model . . .
Grandma . . . loved . . . appreciated . . . respected . . .
    special!

Grandpa Memories

Granddaddy . . . strong . . . protective . . . my papa . . .
Always instructing, unlocking many mysterious
    mechanical sounds;
Repairing the lawn mower, the vacuum, broken
    windows, the train set.
Adjusting carburetors before all the electronic chips.
Sporting a fully outfitted tool belt that could repair
    anything.

Granddaddy . . . strong . . . protective . . . my papa . . .
Reads stories to me complete with sound effects.
Brush burns from whiskers, pungent after shave.
Cheers my sports endeavors, offers pointers.
Recaps the really great game statistics, ancient to
    recent.

Granddaddy . . . strong . . . protective . . . my papa . . .
Recounts all his childhood experiences . . . "Why back in
    my day . . ."
Never reads instructions . . . never asks for directions,
    just plunges ahead.
Always finds the exact tool, gear, nail, nut, or bolt.
But find his blue socks, his keys, or the next roll of toilet
    paper . . . not so easy.

Granddaddy . . . strong . . . protective . . . my papa . . .
Principled, not regimented . . . wise, not degreed . . .
Steadfast patriarch, not choosing to abandon family,
    disciplined, yet still approachable.
Sparse with compliments, but his "You know what I
    mean," speaks volumes.
Granddaddy . . . loved . . . appreciated . . . respected . . .
    special!

Somehow . . . Seems Long Ago

Inseparable as young siblings . . .
A girl/a boy, sister/brother, friends.
Same travel buddies, same interests, same hangouts.
Sat on the front porch together,
Sat on the top concrete step of the row house, side by
    side—together,
Sat on the foot of each other's bed . . . talking . . .
    strangely enough to each other.
Engaged in mischief together and endured the
    punishment together.
Three and a half years difference between birth dates,
    but mutual encouragement, respect, and love.

Somehow . . . seems long ago . . .
As though viewing someone else's dream.

Urban dwelling, father and mother present and
    accounted for.
A hardworking dad, from an island, naturalized long
    before it became fashionable.
Head chef who made $5,500 per year, lived in the ten-
    room house he purchased for his family.
From work brought lobster, beef tenderloin, and other
    discarded tidbits that had been cooked and not
    served, thawed but not used, presented but not
    selected.
This blessing was not truly understood until years
    after-the-fact.

Somehow . . . seems long ago . . .
Wishing the dream could recur.

Stay-at-home-mom, who specialized in taking care of
    her family.
Alabama born, oldest of eight, prepared her well to run
    a household.
No professional aspirations, no personal career plans—
    just provided love, guidance, a listening ear . . .
    encouraged Godliness and cleanliness, simply a
    principled role-model.
Quiet, soft spoken, demure. Because of the cultural
    differences,
    she was always able to curve things her way.

Somehow . . . seems long ago . . .
But, the dream became a nightmare.

Father died, mother's worst fears materialized . . .
Siblings split—one to college, one to the military.
More than half a world apart . . . six years to become
    physically and emotionally disconnected.
Both married, visited the "nest," but at separate times.
Each eventually with one son.
Neither settled in the hometown that both loved.
Life moved on, time passed quickly, the relationship
    between the siblings diminished to nothing.

Somehow . . . seems long ago . . .
A dream from which waking up would be a relief.

Illness invaded mother's being, now at ninety with
    daughter and husband resides.
From the other sibling . . . Letters—none, calls—none,
    visits—none.
What happens to a relationship that was nurtured,
    attended to, and supported?

Where did the caring, the concern, the laughter go?
Was it lost among other actions, travel, or growing up?
Can the giving and sharing, hoping and trusting be
    regained . . .
        so that warmth for, interest in, and love toward one
        another can be rekindled?
How much more time can be wasted waiting?
How much time is guaranteed after ninety years?
How can it be fixed when there is no earthly knowledge
    of how it went wrong in the first place?

Somehow . . . long ago should stay long ago,
    for current rehashing is painful.

Fifty Pearls
(July 5, 1994)

Years are like pearls, unique, precious, and rare.
They take time to cultivate and demand constant care.
Fifty years of marriage is a lifetime blessed with giving,
For two people who rise each day
to engage in complex living.

When the two of you met, how the sparks did fly.
But with no guarantee that they wouldn't die.
You thought you knew all about
your wife/husband-to-be
But information like that was costly—not free.
After marriage, it took time and tears,
long talks and love,
And even that wasn't enough,
were it not blessed from above.
The hard work, even illnesses and making ends meet,
the friends and the good times
were all counted as treats.
Three boys in the nest added life and lots more,
created havoc and fun and challenges galore.

In three different directions, those treasures did go
to exhibit their upbringing of which you did sow.
The old one, the young one, the middle one too,
are all leading lives that point proudly to you.
The family, the caring, the examples you provide
are role-models for others
who have stayed by your side.

Fifty years is a long time to stay on the marriage trail,
But God's blessings and mercy
have helped you prevail.
At this point in your lives,
plan to keep Him firmly there,
So His goodness and His guidance will
hold you gently in His care.

Happy Fiftieth Anniversary

Footsteps after Poe

The plan for life is amazing,
As along God's Grid we glide.
We accomplish so much in one place,
And then to another we slide.
All arrived at that south Raleigh school
Equipped with an unique aptitude.
Each day we gave of that talent and skill
To a complex population did exude.
But the best of times, besides those events,
Were the friendships that were grown.
The respect and support,
the shared laughter and tears
With true caring for each other shown.

We've gone off in different directions,
Years ago would have scoffed at this plan.
That's why Man does not know the future,
For in some places too long would he stand.

Mary Margaret who taught a few children,
How much more to music exists—
Now teaches to thousands who are different
In nooks and crannies she strongly resists.

Joan, still the computer expert,
Who taught, repaired, and launched us all.
Instead of instructing the young ones
Has moved to instruct mega-talls.

Susan, who probably had an inkling
That Spanish was to be a stepping stone,
But for sure she had not the slightest clue
That her family, by one would have grown.

Zon had the vision of a health center at Poe
To make young children more ready for school.
As Fate would have it,
Fate waved its strong hand,
Over all ten centers Zon now rules.

Alice sat quietly as the social studies queen,
Having experienced adventures worldwide.
Decided to snatch the brass ring of happiness,
And with freedom in a dream house resides.

Our stories would make a great novel;
All we need is someone to write
The adventure of friends
At a school with many names.
Book sales would spiral out of sight

Our footsteps have moved us
Away from the "cradle,"
And sent us up life's ladder of success.
Of all the tales that we will remember,
Our friendship will surely be the best!

Tall Black Woman

Who goes there?
Black Woman . . . Tall Black Woman
Strength as a mahogany tree
With a heart like the gentle breezes that rustle through
    its leaves.
An administrative crispness she puts in place—
    Professional when she needs to be,
But professionalism balanced with friendship
    And a sincere caring for people.

Who goes there?
Black Woman . . . Tall Black Woman
Disappointing knees and a frustrating back,
Concealed by determination, organization, and
    persistence.
Expertise in "pre-slugging," buses, books, behavior,
    and observations—
Possessing the ability to say something positive about
    those well thought-out, but didn't-go-the-way-they-
    were-planned lessons.
Offering parents straightforward, honest information
    or disenchanting news about their child with calm
    assuredness.

Who goes there?
Black Woman . . . Tall Black Woman
In white for communion, with praise, and dedication
    to her God,
Allowing her light to be visible for all to see.
Supportive husband and family, she only
    occasionally yearns to return to her mother's
    lap to be soothed as only a mother can do.

But she soothes her five and attempts to meet
    their every need, a never-ending task,
Declining advancement until her oldest is settled,
    the younger has graduated and the youngest
    has appreciatively progressed.

Who goes there?
Black Woman . . . Tall Black Woman
Walking down the path from Poe for the last time—as
    this person.
Her attributes remain, her title has changed.
Life orchestrates these successes so they hurt a little,
    while you grow a lot.
God's speed and blessings to you, Black Woman. You've
    touched many and made a difference.
May you continue to be a Woman of Distinction!

(A Unique Administrator)

Church Family

You see them once or twice a week
And they're not called aunt, uncle, cuz
But in many a moment, both happy & sad,
They stand ready to support total cause.

Church is the family extended part;
Some are held dear and close,
Their prayers & constant intercession
Provide strength & awareness the most.

The calls, the love, the patience
Show God's finger is right there in place,
To take care of hurt, harm, or danger
As from life's tedious plate we must taste.

The church family shares our successes
And dries tears when things don't go well.
What wonder, how caring & giving
These church relatives do always excel.

Thank you to all of the strangers.
Under God's roof you have consented to be—
An extended, supportive church ally,
Providing peace & contentment for me!

Sharing Friends

Section II
The Angel Memorials

He taketh away and creates angels to watch over those left behind. Communication with our angels is accomplished through memories stored in the heart.

Sharing Willie Eugene Haynes
(An Inconspicuous Life)

He was a quiet man, a gentle man.
But his smile stole the hearts of all who met him.

As a child he hung out with his older sister,
Trailing behind her, ignoring his brother
because Al was the baby.
They were always into "something"
around St. Matthews, S.C.
Love of baseball and basketball, as a teen,
made him a good athlete,
and he enjoyed playing both games.
Hunting & fishing pastimes helped him bring
home food for Mom (Simzie) to cook for the family.
"Big Boy," as he was affectionately called,
always tried to be the best.
Working in his Dad's (Marion's) fields,
Willie could pick 200 pounds of cotton
without breaking a sweat, leaving plenty of time
for him to do what he loved—ride the family mule.
His Christian upbringing from years ago,
led him to join First Congregational Church this spring.
He enjoyed the visits from the Deacons,
the Nursing Home Ministry,
& the few members who knew him.
He would raise his finger to recognize a presence . . .
And then there was that smile.

So how do you measure the value of a life?
Is it by how many people one knows?
Or the number of awards won?

It has to do with the heart . . .
and Willie's heart was all it should have been.
Willie's life was unassuming & quiet,
But he was a treasured brother
& an adored human being.

(September 10, 1999)

Bertha Weir—from a Step Away

Our precious Lord took her hand
And led her to a far better land.
He welcomed her gently, and put her at ease
And told her with her life, He was greatly pleased.

He told her he'd planned a time for all things,
And this was a time that her soul should sing.
Imagine her smile as her body was pain free
And in an instant her George, she would again see.

The children aren't there,
But they'd given them their best.
They are ready and able to
Withstand life's toughest tests.
All are strong and caring,
On each other they rely,
For they know their Heavenly Father
Is always close by.

The Lord is their Shepherd
And they will not want.
The memories will sustain them,
Prolonged sadness will not haunt.
The Grands had their share
And their relationship was filled
With visits and cherished moments
And many childhood thrills.
The Great-grand is coming.
Oh, the stories she will hear
Of the strength and commitment of
George and Bertha Weir.
She'll grow and understand

And the legacy will soar,
For her family will enjoy
Contentment and peace evermore.

With Love and Respect to you,
For allowing me, to know your
Parents and Grandparents.

(*November 9, 1997*)

The Round-faced Cutie
(Rev. Willie Williams)

Will our thoughts of him be just a little more distant
now?
How so . . . Heaven instead of Philadelphia?
Absolutely not!
My friend . . . my Round-faced Cutie is still in our
hearts.
With thoughts
No less loving, no less memorable, no less sweet.
He lived according to The Word.
He loved, he guided, he listened, he modeled.
He calmed, he advised, and he encouraged.
Rev. Williams ministered in and out of the pulpit.
In the streets, in the precincts,
In homes, in hospitals and in prisons.
He shared God's Word.
He shared his joy!
He unknowingly provided us with an amplitude
Of precious memories
And extraordinary moments to cherish
And sustain us until we meet again.

Christine Corbin Edger, One Unique Individual

I had a friend, a really best friend who . . .
  —sincerely loved people.
  —enjoyed sitting in the car, in the driveway,
  talking for hours.
  —provided words of wisdom from real experiences.
  —helped many through troubled waters,
    although she was confined to a wheelchair.
  —sought the Lord, waited patiently for His
    response, then acted on His Word.
  —fought battle after battle; personal, medical, and
  societal.
  —loved calling everyone in the church directory to
    share church information.

Christine, who hated to be called that, was . . .
  —completely dedicated to anything she believed in.
  —very sentimental—saved every card she received
    during her fifteen-year illness.
  —devotedly attached to her daughter, Chez
  Michelle.
  —the essence of a virtuous woman, attentive to her
  husband.
  —continually defied medical science because God
    was her doctor.
  —faithful in witnessing to all on how good God had
  been to her.

Chris continued to do things she loved, long after her
    body had given up.
She . . .

    —loved going out to eat and to the movies when
Chez was home.

    —attended church as often as Chez could take
her.

    —intuitively sensed the needs of others and
prayed.

    —always found the time to care about someone
else.

    —was always there for me whether she was at
home, in the hospital, or at the rehabilitation
center.

    —prepared her last Thanksgiving dinner by
herself.

    22-pound turkey in the oven from a wheelchair
. . . difficult, basting turkey during roasting . . .
difficult, once it was ready, removing it . . . not
possible? Chris's prayer: "Lord, please take the
other set of roaster handles and help me get this
turkey to my table . . ." Fantastic dinner!

    Great turkey! Blessed and determined Lady!

A Moment in Time
(Mattie Lewis Farmer)

When we think of the magnitude of time,
life is but a brief moment.
In that brief moment, she was born,
learned, loved, worked, grew
older and departed.
But also in that moment, Mattie Lewis Farmer was
a sister, an aunt, a believer, a friend,
a co-worker, and a neighbor.
In that brief moment, we got to know her moods
and her preferences . . .
her trouble spots and her illnesses . . .
her dedication and her caring . . .
her smile and her laughter.
God watched over her movement through life
and guided her moment in time.
He bestowed her with family, happiness, opportunity,
growth, witness, and peace.
Mattie Lewis Farmer's spot on this earth is empty,
for she has gone on to a far better place.
She will be missed, but she leaves with us
a wealth of memories and cherished moments.
She was a baby sister and the youngest aunt.
She will live on in all our hearts always.

(Sincerely, Mattie's Family)

To Mom from Maika
(18 Years Young)

*I*t was not my plan to leave this place,
A place I truly loved,
*B*ut sometimes plans of humankind
*A*re tempered from above.
I had a vibrant, wonderful life,
*W*ith opportunities galore,
*Y*ou gave me much of life and self,
I could not ask for more.
*Y*ou were role-model, confidante, and friend,
*B*ut more than that, my mom,
*Y*ou worked really hard to protect and defend,
*T*o keep my life's sequence calm.
*W*e both rose early through the years
*T*o support my every endeavor,
*B*e it skating, or basketball, violin or school,
*Y*our words, strength and love failed me never.
*Y*ou provided the sustenance that made me strong,
*F*or much has been packed in my years.
*S*o now is the time to look back and reflect,
*B*ut please let it not be through tears.
*G*od had a plan when He gave us free will,
*A*nd that plan is in place, not in part.
*G*ive God the praise, for I'm with Him now.
*K*eep me empathically tucked in your heart.

With Loving Thoughts of Maika
April 2000

Part 3

Second Thoughts

Because of complexity or phenomenal beauty, many things in this world demand an additional moment of contemplation.

Thoughts

Alone with one's thoughts should bring peace and
     transition,
If the state of the mind is in sound healthy condition.
You can dream, plot, and plan or envision what's in
     store.
For thoughts are not limited by window, wall, or door.
Relive occurrences that once brought great joy
Or foresee the upcoming where you plan to be coy.
Visit with special ones, gone on to their reward,
Recalling love and friendship stopped by death's
     untimely sword.
Thoughts can be deceiving, emitting a false sense of
     hope.
When these invade your processing, search for ways to
     cope.
Allow God to consume your thoughts from the depths of
     Heaven's swells.
The ensuing thoughts will overcome the devil's attempt
     to quell
The positive, the good, the determination to affirm
That God's Word is true and those lessons have been
     learned.
Therefore, it's good to be alone with one's own
     momentous thinking,
To change our world, to find a cure with others'
     thoughts try linking.

Waiting

There must be a secret purpose
    Hidden way down deep somewhere
Where all the things that you hope for
    Are being nurtured and shaped with care.

Those recesses could be a chamber,
    A secret place found in the heart.
Where dreams, hopes, plans, and successes
    Are waiting to realize their start.

What is the trigger that starts the move
    Toward the surface for air?
It's prayers and hopes and supporting friends
    Whose efforts spur faith, not despair.

So waiting does have a purpose,
    For great things must have time to mature.
The more time taken in progress
    Guarantees dreams fulfilled and pure.

A Couple's Understanding . . .
Love is Very Special,
Hard to Find, Hard to Keep!

Love is a very powerful, yet fragile emotion . . .
Love is not the consuming heat of passion.
Love is expandable and all-encompassing . . .
Love is not tightly wrapped around oneself.
Love is a gift from God, given according to His plan . . .
Love is not conjured up with a potion or from a
psychic.
Love is friendship . . .
Between one another and with each other's
acquaintances.
Love is aware of the other's feelings, hopes, and
dreams . . .
Almost without a spoken word.
Love is honest and truthful . . .
Without being accompanied by hurt and put-downs.
Love fosters a special understanding with patience . . .
Even though flare-ups, anger, and disappointments
occur.
Love is forgiving . . .
Knowing that there is no perfect being.
Love is aware that a person cannot change another
person . . .
Believing that only prayer can change anyone or
any situation.
Love is planning . . .
Working under the assumption that there will be a
future.
Love is communicative . . .
Even when there is nothing important to say

Love is being of one accord . . .
    And knowing it deep within your heart.
Love requires daily work . . .
    Making an effort to balance life together and
    expand horizons.
Love is sharing . . .
    A physical, emotional, and spiritual closeness.
Love is two heads thinking as one . . .
    Love is not one head thinking for two.
Love is quiet . . .
    A glance, a touch, a smile, a hug . . . a gentle word.
Love is precious . . .
    But will quickly dissipate if it is neglected.

If you are blessed to experience **it,**
    Love is the most wonderful burden you can carry.

A Single's Understanding . . .
Love is Very Special,
Hard to Balance, Hard to Give!

Love is a strong, yet obscure emotion filled with
potential, bestowed exclusively on all individuals.

Love is a gift from God given in abundance to be used
in abundance.

Love is classified in many ways to be shared
among family, friends, children, and strangers.

Love is a way to connect with the inner spirit of
another being.

Love is not a tool to bully, coerce, or blackmail another
to action.

Love is a conscious acceptance that "Soul Mate"
decisions are guided by the Holy Spirit.

Love is protective, making sure all needs are fulfilled
. . . food, clothing, shelter, and companionship.

Love does not allow one to exist in isolation,
but causes humans to reach out to others.

Love is a closeness not required to be physical,
but warm special feelings shared between people.

Love is a booster, delivered as a hug, a smile, a kind
word or deed.

Love is a flame found deep within, to be cherished,
nurtured, shared, given and received . . . daily.

Love is part of the Master Plan that throughout time,
enlists God as our Comforter, or Companion and
our eternal "Soul Mate."

Engage your Comforter and keep the flame alive!

The Human Response

The road of life does not extend,
    ribbon straight and comfortably wide,
Neither does it remain level and familiar,
    nor offer a safe, sound ride.
Instead the road that we must trod, is filled with twists
    and turns.
Each rumble, pitfall, or stone-cold stop,
    brings lessons that we must learn.
All begin as an infant small, who basically lies and
    waits.
Along come Mom, and/or Dad, with food and shelter
    first rate.

Could this be the human response we seek to define?
    I think not, for that's far too simple.

And what about those teenage years, when
    continual complications ensue?
Is it the teachers, counselors, and shrinks—
    who are hired to see us through?
They say we have so much to do, and there is so little
    time,
We're wrapped into life's massive quest,
    with no strength, our bells to chime.

Could this be the human response we seek to define?
    I think not, for they can be fired.

Adulthood arrives and life is complex,
    filled with decisions through which we must sail,
But are we prepared to catch all of those curves,
    if society's support won't prevail?
If we were to miss even one of those curves,
    we're made to feel we've lost face,
Retreat and regroup are the words that we hear,
    so we rise and return to the race.

Could this be the human response we seek to define?
    I think not, for life's not that harsh.

Along comes the unexpected out of the blue;
    it could be illness, an earthquake or flood.
A tragedy that shakes your very soul,
    causing cold shivers to run through your blood.
One prays to the Father to cure, save, restore,
    though life's unravel seems fulfilled,
During the interlude friends or strangers appear,
    to calm, quiet, serve, and rebuild.

Could *this* be The Human Response that we seek?
    At last it has been found!
The Human Response rises from those who help,
    even though in no way are bound.

Keys! Keys! And More Keys!

Some keys are made of metal
Designed to gain entrance through a door;
There are thousands of them in other places
That do a hundred-fold more.

A smile can be a key of sorts
That opens the human heart.
A pleasant greeting sent straight forth,
A key for conversation to start.

A wink can unlock many things.
Some good and some amiss.
The words "I do" on the other hand
Can unlock wedded bliss.

Accepting the Cross is too a key
That can unlock an imprisoned soul.
With key prayers of the Saints rising up,
Intercession brings solutions untold.

The Lord Himself is the mightiest key
For in Him is found all the best.
Joy, peace, love, long suffering,
Faith, meekness, and gentleness.

For the Little Things . . . Give Thanks

For little things there is no thanks,
    we see, we breathe, we think.
And the more important things, we accept
    with just a wink.
The fact that we can eat and drink and hear
    the birds' sweet song
Is taken for granted every day, we're all
    guilty of this thankless wrong.
There are so many who cannot make,
    the choice to go or stay
Nor can they touch a baby's cheek,
    or join a playful fray.
But we're the first to stand and shout,
    "God send a miracle today!"
"We need to know that You're still there,
    making for us a way."
If we can stop and think and bend, then turn
    to sit and stand . . .
We should lift our eyes to God and raise a
    thankful hand!

Growing and Leaving

You've finished an era of fun and less concern;
You took care of business and much did you learn.
You conquered those steps and graduation has passed;
Now new doors surround but opportunities won't last.

While moving away, in more than one sense,
Surround yourself with Godly things, create a safety
fence.
Check carefully your friends-to-be,
Be sure they're who you need.
As gardens of friends begin to grow,
Take time to daily weed.
Friends are good for doing and sharing,
But some you will find are much too self-caring.
So hang with the ones who are willing to give
And share in the ways that you have learned to live.

At home those you're leaving, will continue to pray
For your learning, success, and safety each day.
That instructors will teach with understandable clarity,
That supervisors/advisors will be helpful . . . a rarity.
Home folk will support with shoulders,
Calls, and cash;
Others will send food for the end-of-month bash.
When a need does occur and no person is there,
Remember that your Heavenly Father is everywhere.
All of your trials, troubles, burdens and fights
Give to Him in their entirety
And your concerns will be light.

We're proud of your accomplishments
And of you for yourself;
Our wish is for continued achievements
And independent wealth.

God bless you, blossoming child,
Summer 2000

Celebrate Something!

When times are tough and life seems rough,
    Celebrate the fact that you belong to God.

When those who supervise have turned a deaf ear,
    Celebrate the fact that God will always hear.

When you organize & plan and things still fall through,
    Celebrate that God's plan does include you.

When long-time true friends have home-gone and left,
    Celebrate the fact that you still have breath.

When life is filled with turmoil & doubt,
    Celebrate the fact that God will work it out.

When at the end of your well-worn rope,
    Celebrate the fact that in God is your hope.

Day in and day out—no matter what life brings,
    Remember God's Promises & Celebrate All Things!

College Is Hard

C	Challenges
O	Obstacles
L	Loneliness
L	Lengthy
E	Experiences
G	Growth
E	Emotional.
I	Intense
S	Searching,
H	Humbling
A	Adjustments,
R	Rewarding
D	Decisions.

College is hard, but definitely worth the effort!

Christmas Is . . .

CHRISTMAS IS . . .

A Unique Birth . . . family . . . cherished memories . . .
giggles . . . children . . . patience . . . fresh snow . . .
sharing . . . hymns . . . favorite recipes and . . .
PEACE

CHRISTMAS IS . . .

Angels . . . decorations . . . living nativities . . . bows . . .
carols . . . mistletoe . . . evergreens . . . visiting
friends . . . hot chocolate and . . . **LOVE**

CHRISTMAS IS . . .

Caring . . . giving . . . calls . . . adults . . . forgiving . . .
scriptures . . . ribbon . . . Matthew I . . . candles . . .
red . . . fir trees . . . candy canes and . . . **HOPE**

CHRISTMAS IS . . .

Snowflakes . . . The Messiah . . . a feeling . . . baked
goods . . . green . . . thoughtfulness . . .
poinsettias . . . fruit, fireplaces . . . wise men . . .
ornaments . . . a star and . . . **JOY**

CHRISTMAS IS . . .

Jesus . . . cantatas . . . Luke 2 . . . smiles . . . home . . .
for the young at heart . . . about others . . . cards . . .
people . . . special . . . and very . . . **REAL**

Finally . . . regardless of income, color, life experiences, education, affiliations, personalities, or ideologies, we all can partake of the amazement and wonder of Christmas.

Someone You Know

Silver atop a mind filled with experience,
knowledge, wisdom and stories.
A face that shows the strength
of many decades . . . perhaps a century.
But yet, a quiet gentleness that goes well with
"Granny" or "Pop-pop," "Nana" or "Gramps."
Marriage at a young age long, long ago,
or marriage in the middle years
—a plannned decision.
And for some, God anointed a more solitary existence
to touch more than one household.
Strong, dark eyes that have witnessed the harsh reality
of
"the back of the bus," or "colored around back,"
"under-funded schools—colored filled."
"Pristine fountains—White only,"
"Inviting lunch counters—White only."
Yes, those eyes have looked into the soul
of segregation and survived.
Broad shoulders on which rested
the burden of being Black,
Struggling to put meat on the table,
shoes on the little feet, an education
into a curious mind.
Sacrificing, working, scrubbing, plowing,
farming, washing, year after year.
But look where we have come . . .
into a new Millennium!
The world is a different place.
Advancements have occurred.
Progress has taken place.
People are the same . . .

life is different,
but continues to be difficult.
Still and all, Praise the Lord! We are Blessed!

By and by

Will we ever understand it better?
When?
Will that be when we are more knowledgeable, more
    mature, more insightful or wise?

The death of healthy young people . . . by and by,
Innocent babes born with death sentences from their
    mothers . . . by and by,
Women repeatedly abused by the ones they love . . . by
    and by,
Thieves who estimate the value of a human life as
    worthless . . . by and by.

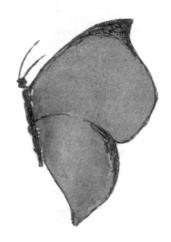

How far away is by and by?
How do we adjust to the lack of patience and the
    ambivalence of acceptance?
What can we do to quicken the pace of understanding?

The sun that rises every morning, seen and unseen . . .
    by and by,
Knowing what's about to be said before its spoken . . .
    by and by,
Clouds that hang so effortlessly against a depthless
    blue sky . . . by and by,
The ongoing life-saving miracles that inhabit our daily
    lives . . . by and by.

Why can't we dwell on the positive?
Why can't we do something about the negative?
Should we pray for understanding sooner?

We are human.
We are imperfect.
We must stand, be patient, and listen.

Besides, what exactly will we do when we do
    understand?

Part 4

Gracefully Silver

Those who are aged and wintry possess the seeds to plant for spring blossoms to bloom. Thank you for cultivating our world.

Aging

The very best way to age
        is to embrace the following and:
    —Age with beauty
     —Age with style
      —Age with humor
       —Age with patience
        —Age with people
         —Age with activity
          —Age with good health
          —Age with youth
           —Age with friends
            —Age with lightheartedness
            —Age with deliberation

              Include all of the above . . .

And you will never have to worry about feeling aged, for
you will be a priceless heirloom!

Senior Through Junior Eyes

Gray hair, aged, statuesque,
Rough hands, knowing face.
Old—never!
Wise and knowledgeable,
Years of pickin', balin', skinnin',
    scrubbin' toilets, washin' someone
    else's clothes, servin' someone else's meals . . .

Holding the family together.
Holding babes in arms.
Holding Bible studies.
Holding prayer court.

Teaching "yes ma'am" and "no ma'am."
Teaching what's right.
Teaching respect and values.
Teaching love by modeling it.

Showed which door, which fountain.
Showed what to do to stay alive.
Showed hope in the future by telling us again
    and again: "Chil', you gonna be sumptin' one day."

That was yesterday.
How we miss yesterday!
How we need *some* of yesterday;
    The bosom, the lap, the comfort, the respect!
Because of yesterday, we have today and today, we *are*
    "sumptin!"
Today we say—Thank You!

Rubies
(Valued, Distinctive, Durable)

How much would you pay for a Senior?
Would you measure in silver or gold?
Experience and knowledge are priceless,
So for what would that model be sold?

A multiple blessing has been granted
To us who have gathered today,
To honor the Seniors before us
In a loving, respectful, and meaningful way.

Emeralds
(Genuine, Treasured, Sought-after)

There's something about the hats, gloves, and smiles
That have the essence of a time now long passed.
The low gentle tones and sincere inquiring eyes
Make us pray that the closeness will last.

A church *can* be measured by those gems at the top,
And by the young feet at the other end.
Care closely for both and the record will show
That First Church's commitment will win.

Sapphires
(Authentic, Top Quality, Long-lasting)

The longer they're with us,
the more precious they should become.
For life runs in repeated tough cycles.
If we are to survive,
their knowledge we must tap,
With respect and not simply trifle.

We know their advice comes straight
from the Word.
For on that for years they have stood.
No matter the topic;
there's experience there
and the counsel that's given is good.

Diamonds

(Most Beautiful, Precious, Rare)

Many treasures in this world
Become more valuable every day;
They're held in very high esteem;
For their well-being, we daily pray.

A look from one can instantly
Make little tykes behave.
The wisdom that these gems possess
Must not be taken to the grave.

Role models all—they have lived the life,
Walked long the narrow line;
They toiled and prayed and rocked and cried
And left their prints in the sands of time.

Aging with Illness

Hours, minutes, seconds tick by,
Slowly, slowly life's on the fly.
Being aware of each moment in time,
Hoping God's clock is not ready to chime.
Tight muscles and tendons, brain messages missing,
Sadness and misery replace former wishing.
Struggle to dress, to feed, just to move,
This ghastly condition has created its grooves.
Unfamiliar at best, independence has gone,
Leaving in its wake, a place that's not home.
It's strange, unrelenting, the spirit is daunted,
Satisfaction elusive, but peace of mind still wanted.

As the days drizzle by, with food hands keep messing,
Eyes start to see illness could be a blessing.
Friends once were there, then too busy to see,
Appear for the long haul, meeting needs one, two, three.
Living day to day, letting life come and go,
Now provides the time to observe Nature's show.
Reliving the values that were stuck in the past,
Accepting now of life, with hope that it lasts.

You've Been Many Places, You've Done Many Things

(1 Timothy 2:8: "I want men and women everywhere to lift up holy hands to God.") (Song of Solomon 7:1: "How beautiful are thy feet. . . .")

You have used those feet for years to bring you to this place. You have used your hands for years to caress, to hold, to build, to applaud. Together these hands and feet have made you special and brought you to this distinguished moment. A place and time to receive appreciation and honor, and be recognized.

Long ago and for some, far away,
God placed you on earth to live, learn, and pray.
The road has been rough, through all kinds of tasks,
And mountains you moved, though many not fast.

Along came the intended, to marry—God's plan,
The flawless dainty woman, the lofty handsome man.
Through the eyes of the beholder, each glowed with sure
    perfection.
Two started down life's winding road, following His
    direction.

You experienced the children with trauma and joy,
The frilly tom-girl, the subdued tough boy.
The money wasn't always there, and finances got real
    thin.
Just when times looked darkest, God's hand and plan
    kicked in.
You learned about life and living, but not from
    expensive degrees,
Instead from worn, tattered pages, of biblically
    referenced decrees.

You saw the wars, depressions too.
You fought the battles and won a few.
The tears flowed freely as ground was gained,
And God only knows how you stood the pain.

As you look back down that road today,
You lift your eyes to heaven and say:
"Thank You, Father, for the blessings You provided . . .
for with your love, grace, and goodness, You surely have
    guided
our feet to this place and our hands to your tasks
with wisdom from life experiences that certainly will
    last."

The upstarts here gathered, salute Seniors today.
You've earned many accolades—with much pride so say.
The wisdom, the knowledge, the determination, and
    peace;
May the will of God bless and His love never cease.

A Solitary Life

How do you measure your solitary life?
Do you measure it by overcome problems and strife?
Do you count the successes, the joys, hurdles crossed?
Do you anguish over the memory of staff that you
    bossed?
Do you savor the triumphs and the people you know,
Or admire the trophies you polish and show?
Do you count mounds of money in slush-fund accounts
And watch all the interest continually mount?
God knows each life by works and by name.
He measures the worth by the good, not the game.
Your life is most precious; it can ne'er be replaced;
Do the best that you can to live under His Grace.

Nowhere to Go

A single solitary soul sitting in the middle of the hall.
Tears running down, no effort made to call.
Snow crowned, rutty skin . . . stiff legs, tight lipped . . .
Huge shiny wheels, around which bony fingers grip.
 Nowhere to go, as life hurries by,
 Nothing to do, but sit there and cry.

Quiet, even silent, conversation long gone,
No interaction, he sits like a stone.
What stories could we attach to this unattended life?
Happiness, sadness, wonderment or strife?
 Nowhere to go, as life hurries by,
 Nothing to do, but sit there and cry.

The time has come, to sit in the hall.
What quality of life does this style we call?
Could no family member volunteer to take him in?
Or would his presence in the home throw all in a spin?
 Nowhere to go, as life hurries by,
 Nothing to do, but sit there and cry.

Did he live his precious life day in and day out,
To end up in a hallway unable to even shout—
That frustration and disappointment have consumed
  his tired soul,
So all that's left is abandonment and sadness untold.
 Nowhere to go, as life hurries by,
 Nothing to do, but sit there and cry.

God's Senior Angels

Active seniors to and fro,
Blessing others as they go.

Busy, busy things to do,
Lists of tasks, not just a few.
Not a lot of money to share,
But more than that is just to care.
To drive the disabled around the city,
To senior activities, without a moment's pity.
Cards and remembrances regularly sent,
Sitting and chatting—important time spent.
For outings some can go, if help comes for dressing,
Seniors helping seniors is truly a blessing.
It's great to keep the elders in the mainstream of
      things,
To enjoy and share the intrigue each opportunity
      brings.

Active seniors to and fro,
Blessing others as they go.

Part 5

Sensitively Pensive

Delicate reflection can elucidate confusing moments and intensify the desire to hope, to dream and to create.

Summer . . . God Is So Good!

School ends . . . Students graduate . . .
Marriages begin . . .
God Is So Good!

Flowers bloom . . . Sweet fragrances rise . . .
Insects abound . . .
God Is So Good!

Travel plans . . . Moving here & there . . .
In spite of dangerous highways . . .
God Is So Good!

Warming weather . . . Sunny Skies . . .
Brief showers . . .
God Is So Good!

Celebration of the Fourth . . .
Visits from coast to coast . . .
Family reunions . . .
God Is So Good!

Traditional season for relaxation . . .
Pastors' revitalization time . . .
Pulpit guests . . .
God Is So Good!

Matters not what's happening . . .
Matters not where you are . . .
Matters only that it's understood . . .
That God Is So Very Good!

Honor God

Honor God with thanks
. . . for being there
. . . for peace
. . . for health
. . . for protection
. . . for boldness
. . . for quietness
. . . for closeness
. . . for salvation
. . . for a listening ear
. . . for answered prayer
. . . for fellowship
. . . for dedication
. . . for new beginnings
. . . for safe passage
. . . for rest
. . . for strength
. . . for opportunities
. . . for forgiveness &
. . . for still another chance!

Jesus, Our All-in-All

Do you ever look around and find,
  No one is even there?
Look to Jesus and you'll see,
  He's really everywhere!

When shades of gray descend on you,
  And color your view of things,
Look to Jesus and you'll feel
  The joy that He can bring!

Those heartaches, troubles pressing down,
  With weight too much to bear;
Call on Jesus and you'll know
  That He sincerely cares!

For sleepless nights and endless days,
  And valleys that seem really low,
Pray to Jesus and you'll find
  mountaintop experiences grow!

Some troublesome worries may produce doubt,
  But the message's so plain to see.
Be still and quiet, listen and believe;
  In Jesus your comfort will be!

What Does It Take?

What does it take to <u>Praise the Lord?</u>
    —A sincere and joyous heart.
What does it take to <u>Love the Lord?</u>
    —A confession's a good place to start.
What does it take to <u>Bless the Lord?</u>
    —A commitment from deep within.
What does it take to <u>Thank the Lord?</u>
    —Appreciation to Him as your friend.
What does it take to <u>Trust in the Lord?</u>
    —Daily devotion to His Word.
What does it take to <u>Wait on the Lord?</u>
    —Understanding that all prayers are heard.
What does it take to <u>Sing for the Lord?</u>
    —A spirit-filled melodious song.
What does it take to <u>Walk with the Lord?</u>
    —A conscious effort that lasts the day long.

Never Give Up!

Never give up the best laid plan,
God's angels will help you achieve.
Things may look bleak to the naked eye,
But prayer will help you succeed.
It will be done with peace and calm,
His promises He keeps still.
Wait patiently with confidence,
And supplications He will fulfill.

So never give up and never give in,
For God knows exactly how, where, and when.
We need to hold fast to that heavenly view
Then stumbling blocks will be a paltry few.
Be strong! Be defiant! Put Satan's lies under your feet.
With God's Word and solid belief, bad times are
    permanently beat.

. . . Pressing On

Pain, throbbing, disease,
Fear, diagnosis.
By His stripes we are healed.
. . . Press on

Money, no money,
Bills, collections, wants,
Shortcomings, repairs.
God will supply all of my needs.
. . . Press on

Job, worldliness, stress,
School, demands, turmoil.
God provides a peace that passes
all understanding.
. . . Press on

Loneliness, abandonment,
Depression, hurt, disappointment.
Let not your heart be troubled . . .
Lo, I will be with you always.
. . . Press on

Hypocrisy, confusion, battles,
Mountains, disagreements.
The Lord thy God will hold thy right
hand, saying fear not; I will help thee.
. . . Press on

We: Praise, Worship, Exalt, Glorify, Honor, Revere, & Adore . . . God
He Gives: *Love, Mercy, Blessings, Joy, Grace,* Forgiveness, & Compassion

We are gratefully, Pressing On

Hope Rises

Will Occur Again Tomorrow · · · · · · · · · SUNRISE!

Extends No Patent
    Grants Daily Diversity
      Brightens Spirits
        Affords Possibilities

Suggests Potential Success
    Bequeaths A Warming Glow
      Defines A Time
        Offers Opportunity

Displays Unspeakable Beauty
    Shows God's Smile
      Emits Gentle Light
        Is Cloaked In Soft Color
          Enjoys Worldwide Fame

SUNRISE · · · · · · · · · · · · · · · · · Guarantees

      A New Beginning.

Stormy Weather

Trees bent low, sweeping the ground
    with fingerlike extensions.
Some lie prone having lost the fight;
    they plead for quick redemption.
A wind whips round, shear force the
    sightless funnel's circular path,
Unnerves the strong and displays a
    side of God's untamable wrath.
Rain pelts down through lightning fierce,
    each drop a knife point's prick,
Thunder's shattering claps descend to earth
    through gray clouds rolling thick.
These storms of life come frequently,
    rage wild and out-of-control,
What can we do to protect ourselves
    and save our slothful souls?
Pray, praise, worship, sing,
    bless His name each day whole.
Stay in the Word, His angels seek,
    and He will save your soul!

Part 6

Secret Closet

Communication Central—a place that allows the expression of feelings, supplications and praise to a Mighty God. A place to hear His voice.

A Prayer—Pressing On

Gracious Lord, sometimes along our journey of life, we find ourselves wedged into a corner, forgetting our heritage. Forgetting that You have said, we are your ancestry. Let us stand using that fortification. Allow us to persevere and be patient in times of frustration.

Father, grant us the serenity and calm assurance needed to hear You. Open our hearts so that we can prayerfully communicate with You and experience your presence. Clear our thinking, Lord, so You can renew us through your promises. Strengthen our faith, and keep us pressing on. Amen.

A Prayer—Golden

Lord God, we sense your presence as your spirit moves among us on this Sabbath morning. The sun has acknowledged another day for which we thank You. We come with purpose. We feel the unity of family and extended family; men, women, children, friends, and beloved elders, as we gather to pray and worship collectively.

Accept the praise we bring and the recognition of our continuing need for your forgiveness and direction. Thank You, God, for those whose years have been extended into the revered echelon of life. Touch us all with your grace and mercy, as we strive to do your will. Amen.

Putting on the Full Armor of God
A Spiritual Resource

O Lord, we give You quiet intervals to show our thanks and sing Your praises.

We give You our work, knowing that You will use it to fulfill Your purposes.

We give You our time, asking You to guide us in what is good and acceptable and perfect.

We give You our friends and families, seeking to follow Your example of how to love and bless them.

We give You our lives, trusting that You will not forsake the work of Your hands.

All that we are, and all the we have, is Yours.

Receive it to your glory and praise, through Jesus Christ our Lord. Amen.

The Christmas Prayer

Bright and gentle was the night
When a star appeared to mark the sight.
The voice of angels became the horn
To announce to the world,
that the Savior was born.
We want to remember why He was sent.
The meaning, understanding,
and exactly what it meant.
It wasn't for shopping, decorations,
or hurried strife
But for peace on earth and eternal life.
God gave the greatest gift of all
And it was not found at a shopping mall.
This is the season to give from the heart,
Remembering the Christmas story
is the best place to start.
Dear God, allow us to praise Your name
To praise You for Jesus who ultimately came
To follow Your plan, to execute Your Word,
To give us the story each year to be heard.
So as we retire to arise Christmas Day,
With joy and fulfillment
and the awareness to say—
Thank You, Dear God, for the gift
of The Holy One,
Baby Jesus, the King of Angels,
Your Only begotten Son!

Woven

How precious is the life that You, Father, have given.
The dawning of each day brings renewed
appreciation of Your awesome presence.
The burning desire that makes daily
interactions, activities, and
responsibilities palatable, is
energized by the fact that

ALL THAT IS NEEDED,
YOU HAVE ABUNDANTLY PROVIDED.

The guidance for life's challenges and successes
is intertwined with the knowledge of *Your Will and
Your Way*. My soul is filled with gratitude for
the blessings You have bestowed; for
strength and stamina, the ability to
discern and delineate, plus the
capacity to love and care.

Praise be to God!

With loyal conviction, understanding is sought.
With humble obedience,
trust in Your Word is held steadfast.
With unshakable faith,
this pilgrim offers adoration,
holy worship, and praise.
Praise You, Father, for all that
You have woven into my life's
pattern. Amen

Recapture the Moment

Cold, clear, crisp air,
Stars that create thousands
of multifaceted sparkles in the ebony
sky. Visible moisture droplets float upward
toward the brilliant Star in the East.
Sounds of amazement can be
heard from the sloping
hills of the meadowland.
Robed in common woolen garb in one field, and
fine linen piped in gold lamé on a crest in another.
They point, they raise their hands in awe.
Feeling drawn eastward, but filled with uncertainty
until the messenger proclaims the Birth.
Unspeakable joy, anticipation, peace,
promise and goodwill fill the hearts of man.
A perfect moment choreographed by God!
How extraordinary it would be, to revisit
that impeccable moment once more!

A Prayer—After the Hurricane

Almighty Father, we know that our strength comes from You. Therefore, it is not hard for us to share, to do, to give or to pray for our neighbors. You have defined neighbors as anyone whose needs we can meet. The needs are so great after the devastating storm, that sometimes we become overwhelmed. But You have said, to not be weary in well-doing; for we know that in due season, we shall reap, if we faint not.

We bless You, Lord, for allowing us to bear one another's burdens without fainting. Therefore, let us not ignore the pain. Allow us to be compassionate and not selfish, empathetic and not inconsiderate, charitable and not covetous. Remembering, that all is not physical; we must also respond to the loneliness, the despair, the fatigue, and the bereavement. We thank You, Lord, for guiding us to accept the opportunity and responsibility of assisting our brethren in need.

So we come to Praise! We Come to Thank! We Come to Bless! Amen.

September Prayer

Precious Father, in these hectic days and times, guide our thoughts in making our "Just a Few More Things" lists worthy tasks for the uplifting of Your kingdom. Keep us from becoming pressed down with worthless assignments. Six days shall we labor for our daily existence, but allow us to also work, throughout those days, toward Your understanding and with Your guidance.

Then, on your precious Seventh Day, let us know that if our labors do not include You, The Lord Our God, we labor in vain. We know that no matter how hard we work, nothing good and wholesome can come to us, without knowing You. Let this Labor Day weekend remind us of *your* promises and *our* responsibilities. Labor Day is not our day of rest, but rather another day to praise and be thankful that we can work and do all things through You, who gives us strength. Bless us and grant us Your special peace. Amen.

Daily Prayer
(To The Holy One, we give thanks and praise.)

We bless Your name, O God.
We know that our lives are in Your hands.
We look around each day that our eyes are blessed to
open
and see all that You have fashioned,
from the smallest miracle to the most grand prophecy.
We stand in awe of Your power and Your might;
Your grace and Your peace;
Your love and Your gentleness.
We invite You into our temples—
each different, but each needy.
Continue to support us through
the network of family, friends,
co-workers, acquaintances, even strangers
that You have established around our lives.
For any or all of them can deliver
a message or reminder from You to us.
Gift us Your protection, guidance, and ability to grow—
regardless of our age.
For we know that You ask us not
to bear more than our shoulders can carry.
Amen.

You have come to the end of
The Butterflies' Path.
May it prove to be the beginning
Of "something" Beautiful.